THE BODY
God's Design

written by
Monica Ashour & Patrick Gordon

illustrated by
Gary Undercuffler

Level 3
BOOK 1
Second Edition

 **TOBET** THEOLOGY OF THE BODY EVANGELIZATION TEAM

Dedicated to the Church, including our family and friends, and especially to Mother Mary and Saint John Paul.

Tremendous thanks to all TOBET members over the years. Special thanks to Andrea, Kathy, Sarah, Sheryl, Tamara, and Véronique. We are grateful for consultation work by the translator of the *Theology of the Body*, Dr. Michael Waldstein, as well as Dr. Susan Waldstein and Dr. Danielle M. Peters. We are also grateful for the consultation work of Katrina J. Zeno, MTS.

For Caryn

Nihil Obstat: Tomas Fuerte, S.T.L.
Censor Librorum

Imprimatur: +Most Reverend Samuel J. Aquila, S.T.L.
Archbishop of Denver
Denver, Colorado, USA
Feast of Divine Mercy
April 24, 2022

Library of Congress information on file. ISBN 978-1-945845-40-6 • Second Edition
Cover Design: FigDesign • Layout: Emily Gudde • Editor: Dayspring Brock • Associate Editor: Alexis Mausolf
First Edition written by S.C. Ashour & Tamara Kuykendall

Excerpts from the English translation of the *Catechism of the Catholic Church*. New York: Catholic Book Publishing Co., 1994.
Based on John Paul II's *Man and Woman He Created Them: A Theology of the Body*. Trans. Michael Waldstein, Copyright © 2006. Used by permission of Pauline Books & Media, 50 Saint Paul's Ave, Boston, Massachusetts 02130. All rights reserved. www.pauline.org.
All Scripture verses are from the *New American Bible*, Revised Edition (NABRE).
Excerpts from *YOUCAT*. Trans. Michael J. Miller. (San Francisco: Ignatius Press, 2011), www.ignatius.com. Used with permission.
The quote on p. 40 is from Pope Benedict XVI. *Benedictus*. Ed. Rev. Peter John Cameron, O.P.
(San Francisco: Magnificat/ Ignatius Press, 2006), www.ignatius.com. Used with permission.

Printed in the United States of America. © Copyright 2022 Monica Ashour. All rights reserved. No part of this book may be reproduced or transmitted in any form or by any means, electronic or mechanical, including photocopying, recording, or by any information storage and retrieval system without permission in writing from the publisher.

Table of Contents

1 ## God the Master Artist   4
- God, the Master Artist, designed everything in the world.
- God designed everything with a certain nature.
- God designed human nature in His image.

2 ## Receiving God's Loving Design   14
- God lovingly designs everyBODY.
- It is good that God designed human nature with limits.
- By living according to God's design, we can be fully alive.

3 ## God, Me, and Identity   26
- God gives each person a unique identity that is connected to human nature.
- A person's identity is always connected to a mission for love.
- Obeying God's design allows persons to discover and live out their true identity.

4 ## Trinity Identity   38
- Through Baptism, every person is given a supernatural Trinity Identity.
- The saints are models who live out their true identity.
- The greatest superpower of the saints is doing small things with great love.

God the Master Artist

Creation: God's Masterpiece

JP loves to visit museums to see the wondrous paintings. He knows some are masterpieces painted by master artists.

JP is a boy who also loves to paint. He wants to grow up to be a great artist. He loves making paintings of wild animals, especially bears and beavers and bison.

Did you know that God is also an artist? He is the Master Artist Who shaped and colored all of creation —including **you**!

This means that the whole world is like a museum full of beautiful, living masterpieces.

"The heavens declare the glory of God; the firmament proclaims the works of his hands." *Ps. 19:1*

Natures: Designed by God

God carefully planned each of His masterpieces. He designed everything in creation to have a certain nature.

God designed water to be wet. This is the nature of water. He made wildflowers to have colorful petals. This is the nature of all flowers.

He designed dogs to bark and wag their tails. This is the nature of all dogs.

Mike marvels at how God made cheetahs.
A cheetah can run faster than Mike because of its nature.
It is designed for speed.

Each Body Has a Design

God designed bears to hibernate, frogs to capture flies, and bees to make honey.

Each creature's **body** reveals its nature by the way it looks, the things it can do, and what it has in common with other creatures of the same kind.

God's design for a bear's body lets it store food for hibernating.

God designed frog bodies with long legs for hopping and sticky tongues for catching flies.

God designed bees with bodies that can make honey.

Each **body** reveals its wonderful design and true nature.

"[The human person], though made of body and soul, is a unity."
CCC 382

God's Design for Human Nature

What does the **human body** teach about **human nature**? God designed human bodies with ears for hearing, legs for walking, and eyes for seeing. That's part of human nature.

God made human nature in His image: body **and** spirit. Maggie can dance, play sports, sing, laugh, and pray. Her bodily actions show she has a spirit too.

How else did God design human nature? To be with others.

It's human nature to pray to God.
It's human nature to be in a family.
It's human nature to have friends.
It's human nature to tell stories.
It's human nature to love others.

Designed **for** Each Other

All human persons share the same human nature; the human body teaches this truth. That means human persons **belong** to each other, especially families.

It would be strange if Mike thought a bear was his mom, or a frog was his sister, or that he should make honey like a bee. He recognizes everyBODY in his human family. They are gifts **for** each other.

Because of their bodies, Maggie and Grandma can hug. Because of his body, Isaac can be a gift to his sister by kicking a beach ball to her.

Because of his body, Maggie's uncle can be a scientist who discovers new medicines. Because of his body, JP can receive the Gift of Jesus' Body at Mass.

JP prays, "I love You, my God."

# 2 Receiving God's Loving Design

God's Masterpiece

Watching the artist at work, Kathleen wonders about God's plan for everyBODY. She realizes how God the Master Artist carefully planned His design of human nature.

God is like a Divine Painter who loves Kathleen and every one of His masterpieces.

"Out of the surplus of his love he created us."
YOUCAT 2

It would be silly if a painting tried to tell a master artist what and how to paint!

Sadly, some people think God makes mistakes. But God carefully plans each person as a masterpiece.

Kathleen accepts God's loving design for everyBODY with a grateful heart.

God's Design Is Best

Helen ponders what might happen if creatures could reject the nature that God gave them:

"What if stars grew legs and walked away? Then I'd never be able to look at the amazing night sky."

"What if the colorful flowers in my garden decided to become skunks? I'd lose my lovely, sweet-smelling garden."

"What if my dog, Spot, tried to be a world leader? I'd lose him as a pet."

Obeying God's Good Design

Alex ponders what would happen if humans disobeyed God's design:

"If my mom decided to become a unicorn, she wouldn't be able to understand me."

"If I replaced my hands with claws, I'd injure my friends."

"What if human persons tried to become machines? They'd lose the best gift of all—love!"

"Give me understanding to keep your law, to observe it with all my heart. Lead me in the path of your commandments, for that is my delight."   Ps. 119:34-35

Living within Limits

JP reflects on God's design for his human body. He is learning that his human nature has certain limits.

"Because of my body, I need a bath to stay clean. Because of my body, I need food, water, and sleep for strength and energy. Because of my body, I need my dad to help me cross the street."

It would be harmful to JP if he chose never to bathe, eat, sleep, or drink water—or to run out into the street. His human limits remind him of his need for God and his family.

JP prays, "God, it's hard to accept my human limits and obey Dad when I want to run and play. Please help me to obey."

Real Life, Real Adventures

Sometimes Isaac does not feel like accepting God's limits. He'd rather escape into a virtual world.

But then Isaac remembers that a virtual world is not real life; he is not an avatar in a video game.

God's plan for Isaac is to experience real life through the gift of his body. He trusts God's design and plays outside with his family.

As he plays, Isaac realizes he loves being outside, splashing in the water, and building sandcastles.

Because he is present to the real world through his body, Isaac gets to share joy and laughter.

Isaac prays, "God, thank You for helping me live within the limits of Your design so that I can be fully alive and happy!"

"So God created mankind in his image… male and female he created them." Gen. 1:27

God Designed Girls

Emma ponders God's plan for girls. Emma accepts God's gift of her girl body. She will not grow up to be a horse or a man or a computer.

Emma can play make-believe that she is a horse, but that's not real life. Emma knows that her loving Father, the Master Artist, designed her to grow up to be a woman, made to help others.

"The human body shares in 'the dignity of the image of God.'"
CCC 364

God Designed Boys

Isaac ponders God's plan for boys. Isaac accepts God's gift of his boy body. He will not grow up to be a rock or a woman or a dragon.

Isaac can play a virtual reality game, pretending to be a dragon, but that's not real life. Isaac knows that his loving Father, the Master Artist, designed him to grow up to be a man, made to help others.

23

Love Is God's Ultimate Design

God the Father, Son, and Holy Spirit all love each other perfectly. God designed humans in His own image and likeness. This means human persons, too, are created for love.

Since human persons are designed this way, they can only be happy and live fully when they give and receive love. The best way to do this is to be a gift to others.

Alex, Kathleen, and Tien give and receive love in friendship through the reality of the body. They realize that there's no better gift than being bodily present to each other.

They walk in the woods, tell stories, joke around, and race each other. By living out God's plan, they enjoy the gift of each other's uniqueness. They are fully alive!

3 God, Me, and Identity

God's Unchanging Gifts

God, the Master Artist, designed you to have your own identity. Your identity is who you are as a unique person. Identity is always connected to God's good design.

Because of God's design, Tony and Tien can each recognize their own personal identity. They each have a human body; this reveals their identity as human persons. That's God's unchanging gift.

Tien knows she has a girl body. This reveals her identity as a girl. That's God's unchanging gift.

Tony knows he has a boy body. This reveals his identity as a boy. That's God's unchanging gift.

EveryBODY is designed with a mission to love God and others. That's God's unchanging gift too!

My Family and My Identity

The human body is God's message that persons belong with each other. Our identity is rooted in our relationship with God and others, especially our parents.

Kyle knows that a part of his identity is to be a loving son and brother. He accepts his identity by doing his chores. His identity is tied to the gift of self.

Christine knows that a part of her identity is to be a loving daughter and sister. She accepts her identity when she enjoys a piggyback ride from her dad. Her identity is tied to the gift of self.

Kyle and Christine learn more of who they are when they receive their parents' love. That's God's unchanging gift as well.

> "Through his Word, he pours into our hearts the Gift that contains all gifts, the Holy Spirit." *CCC 1082*

Uniquely Me!

Even though all people share the **same** human nature, this does not mean that everyone is identical. God gives each person a **special** identity. Each human is a unique person.

Emma, Kyle, and JP trust that God made each of them special. As they grow and act according to God's good design, they discover more about what makes each of them unique.

Emma expresses her unique identity through her gift of music and by being a great friend.

Kyle has special gifts for drawing and telling funny jokes. JP lives his identity by teaching baseball to kids with special needs.

God wants us to discover our special gifts and unique identity.

Emma's Identity and Mission

Emma wants to live according to her true, God-given identity. She realizes that one of her special gifts is noticing those who are left out.

How can Emma use this gift for her mission to love? She sees Maggie alone at lunch. So Emma goes to sit at the cafeteria table with Maggie. They become friends.

Emma prays, "God, thank You for my gifts and for my new friend."

Isaac's Identity and Mission

Isaac wants to live according to his true, God-given identity. Isaac knows he's really good at science.

How can he use this gift for his mission to love? He works hard in class so that one day when he is a vet, he will help sick animals. He follows God's mission for his life.

Isaac prays, "Thank You, God, for helping me improve my talents and for leading me on an adventure!"

"But God... is rich in mercy, because of the great love he had for us...."   *Eph. 2:4*

Love Leads to Identity

Mike finds his full identity by following his God-given mission to love—to be a gift for others.

Mike better understands his identity as a son when he makes dinner with his dad. When he tells stories to classmates and prays for them, he sees his identity as friend.

Unfortunately, Mike acts against his true identity when he sins.

Mike remembers times when he cheated in games and said mean things to friends. Sinning makes it harder for Mike to understand who he is, but sin does not change his identity. He is always a person made in God's image.

When he repents and receives God's loving mercy, Mike can more easily discover his unique identity and live joyfully.

"[T]he church of the living God [is] the pillar and foundation of truth."

1 Tim. 3:15

The Church and True Identity

Maggie knows that people find their true identity by obeying God's design of human nature.

However, Maggie sees people making bad decisions and sometimes feels confused about her own identity and mission.

Maggie's parents explain that the Catholic Church is God's loving guide for living out her true identity.

God's rules limit Maggie's choices, but that's a good thing! By following His plan, she won't choose the wrong path. Maggie still has many ways she can live out her mission to love.

Maggie prays, "God, I don't know yet what I am going to do when I grow up. I'm so excited to discover Your holy will!"

37

4 Trinity Identity

Trinity Identity: Tien

Tien gratefully receives God's loving plan for her. She is a person, a girl, and a daughter. Those are God's unchanging gifts.

Another unchanging gift is that God will **always** love Tien and each person He has created.

But God wants to be even closer to persons, so He offers the special gift of Baptism to all.

When Tien was baptized, she received her identity from the Holy Trinity. She is a beloved daughter of God the Father, a sister to Jesus, and a temple of the Holy Spirit.

This means Tien is a Catholic Christian. She belongs to God. Her Trinity Identity is God's unchanging gift to her.

Tien prays, "Thank You, Father, for giving me my deepest identity—I am Your beloved daughter."

Trinity Identity: Tony

Tony gratefully receives God's loving plan for him. He is a person, a boy, and a son. Those are God's unchanging gifts.

Tony knows that God loves him; he is the Master Artist's masterpiece.

God will **always** love Tony as His own. Tony belongs to God. Tony knows that his Trinity Identity is God's unchanging gift to him.

It's so thrilling how everyBODY is called to be like Jesus, yet each person remains an unrepeatable gift.

Pope Benedict XVI once said: "We see how Thérèse of Lisieux or Saint John Bosco or Edith Stein... has learned from Jesus how to go about being human.... All these people have become truly like Jesus—[but] they are also [unique] and original" (*Benedictus*, 44).

Tony prays, "Thank You, Father, for giving me my deepest identity—I am Your beloved son."

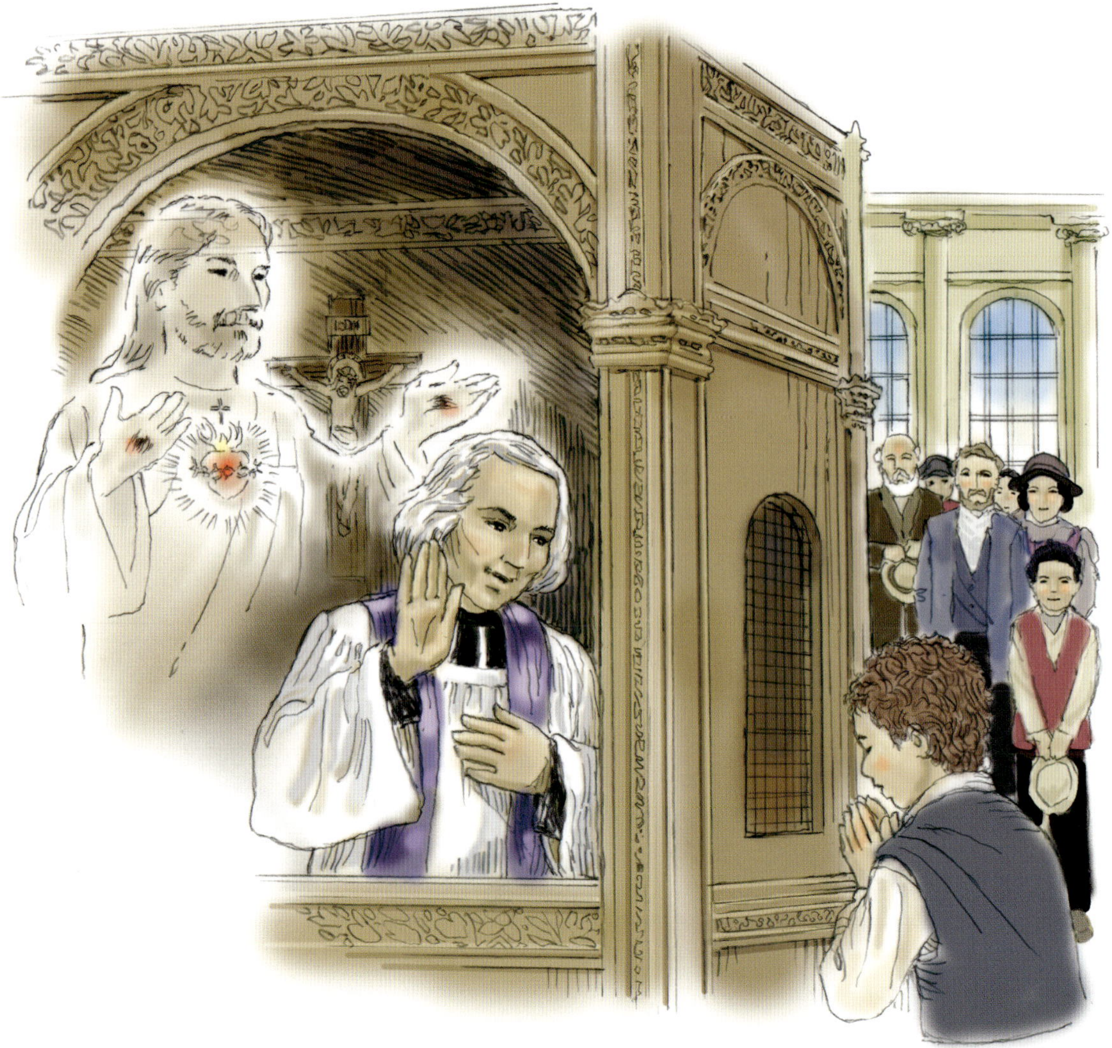

> "…[T]he risen Christ entrusted to the apostles the power to forgive sins when he gave them the Holy Spirit."
>
> CCC 984

Superpower: St. John Vianney

Tien wonders how to live according to her Trinity Identity. She looks to the saints who understood and lived out their Trinity Identity, rooted in God's love.

St. John Vianney knew he would always be loved by God. Even though he wasn't good in school—he failed many classes and people made fun of him—St. John Vianney embraced his Trinity Identity.

With help from the Master Artist, St. John Vianney worked on his gift of listening to others. God then made this his superpower!

St. John Vianney received his superpower, gladly hearing Confessions for hours. What a gift to represent Jesus and forgive sins! People grew in holiness because of his gift; superpowers are meant to lead people to Jesus.

Superpowers of Super Saints

Tony is amazed at the things the saints could do, having received their identity from the Trinity.

St. Teresa of Ávila was so devoted to prayer and her relationship with the Trinity, that God gave her the superpower of levitation (floating in the air)!

Through her holiness, God grants us a glimpse of Heaven. She lived out her Trinity Identity.

St. Padre Pio was so committed to serving others that he was given the superpower of bilocation (being in two places at once)!

God gave him the super-ability to bring Jesus to more than one person at a time. He lived out his Trinity Identity.

The saints have complete trust in God's love. This can bring about supernatural wonders.

45

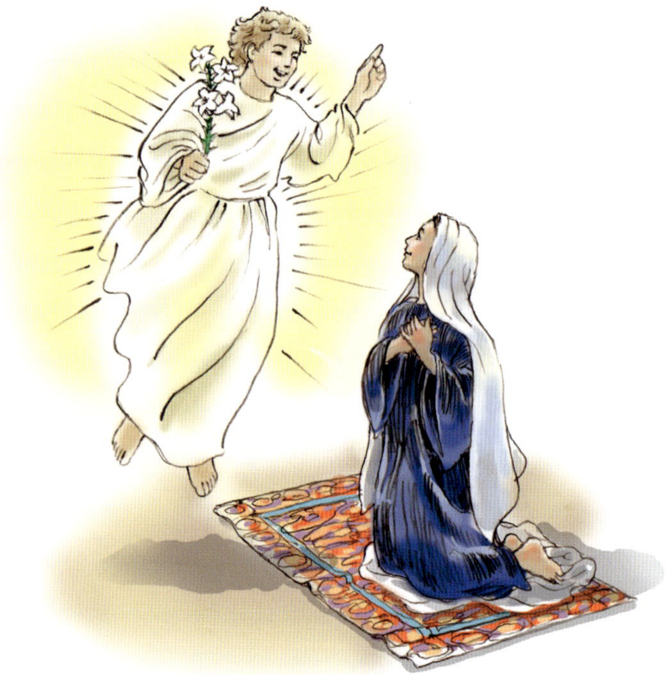

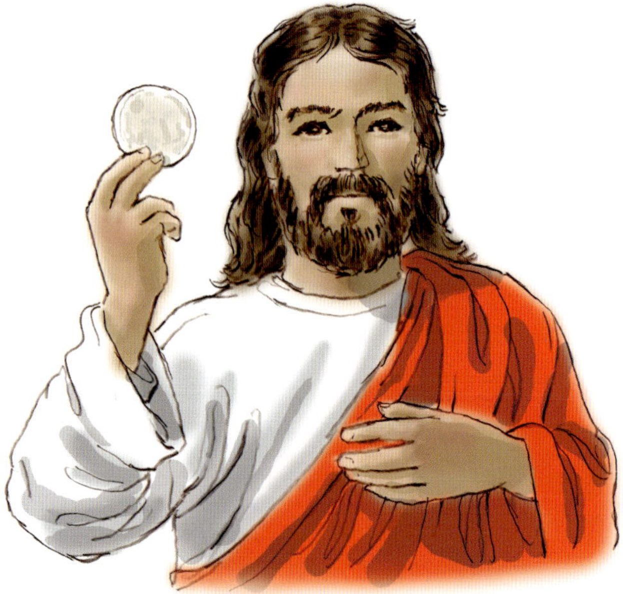

> "Therefore the child to be born will be called holy, the Son of God." *Lk. 1:35*

Small Things with Great Love

"But I can't possibly be a great saint or have a superpower," says Tony. "Neither can I," says Tien. They need not worry.

Most saints have the superpower of doing **small** things with **great** love. Mother Mary's "little" act of saying "Yes" to God brought about the greatest gift there is to the world: Jesus.

Tony and Tien can imitate Mary's super-ability to love by receiving Jesus' Gift of Himself in the Eucharist. This helps them to do small things with great love.

This is what makes someone a saint. This is how saints live their mission. This is why everyBODY can be a saint!

Trinity Identity for Eternity

Your deepest identity is rooted in being loved by God as His own child.

The Master Artist designed you and everyBODY with a special talent, mission, and superpower to bring His Love to the world.

As you receive God's loving Trinity Identity, you will become fully alive now, and for all eternity!